Beginning Level

English Through Citizenship

Elaine Kirn
West Los Angeles College

Delta Systems Co., Inc.

First Edition

9 8 7 6 5 4 3 2

Published in The United States by Delta Systems Co., Inc..

ISBN 0-937354-38-4

Manufactured in the United States of America

Series Design and Production: Etcetera Graphics, Canoga Park, CA

Typesetting: Words and Deeds, Glendale, CA
Artist: Terry Wilson (Etcetera Graphics)

ACKNOWLEDGEMENTS

Thanks to the amnesty coordinators and instructors of the Los Angeles Community College District and surrounding schools for supporting this project and offering helpful suggestions, as well as to Victoria Richart of Los Angeles Mission College and the Los Angeles and Orange County curriculum committee for the creation of complete course outlines and guidelines. Special appreciation goes to Jon Hendershot of Los Angeles Southwest College and Jack Fujimoto of the LACCD for initiation of the project.

And as usual, thanks to a hard-working staff and freelancers:
John Dermody for research and initial drafts, John Millrany and
Pat Campbell for editing, Terry Wilson for expressive artwork,
Suzette Mahr for typesetting, Anthony Thorne-Booth for falling in love with the new computer, Chuck Alessio for putting it all together, and all of us for long, long workdays and evenings.

In advance, appreciation goes to Dick Patchin of Delta Systems and the sales staff for enthusiasm and being out there.

Contents

Contents

To the Student

Are you just beginning your study of English? Do you want to learn about the customs, government, and history of your new country, state, and city in easy English? Then the Beginning Level of *English Through Citizenship* is the right level for you.

The information in this book will help you prepare for an Immigration and Naturalization (INS) examination for permanent residence or citizenship. You can study the information on your own. To check your answers, look at the Answer Key of the Beginning Level Instructor's Manual.

You may also use this book in a course in English as a Second Language at a public or private school. This course will include instruction in government and history. You can learn basic vocabulary and information from *English Through Citizenship* before you try to read more difficult books in English.

If the language in the Beginning Level of *English Through Citizenship* is very easy for you, you can learn more vocabulary and information from the Intermediate Level.

To the Instructor

English Through Citizenship is a three-level program of simplified civics material for speakers of English as a Second Language.

The Beginning Level of *English Through Citizenship* is designed for individuals literate in their native languages who have just begun to learn English. A score between 165 and 190 on the CASAS (California Adult Student Assessment System) or a comparable score on another English language skills placement test indicates that an individual is likely to succeed with the materials at this level.

English Through Citizenship is based on curriculum outlines developed by the Los Angeles Community College District (LACCD) and the Los Angeles County Community College Consortium for Amnesty (LACCCCA). These outlines have been approved by the California State Department of Education and the Immigration and Naturalization Service for implementation in classes funded by State Legislative Impact Assistance Grants (SLIAG) in accordance with the Immigration Reform and Control Act (IRCA).

The information in the program is derived largely from three texts issued by the federal government: *United States History 1600-1987*, *U.S. Government Structure*, and *Citizenship Education and Naturalization Information* (U.S. Department of Justice, Immigration and Naturalization Service, 1987).

Based on proven ESL methodology in language skills instruction (primarily listening, speaking, and reading), *English Through Citizenship* will benefit individuals applying for legalization status as permanent residents of the United States or for U.S. citizenship. It is also appropriate for general civics instruction in high schools and colleges.

The history, government, and citizenship material of the program is divided into twelve numbered units, each subdivided into several lettered modules. Each module consists of four pages of material, designed for one or more class periods of instruction with follow up (homework and/or review).

For a complete listing of the material available at all three levels, see the Instructor's Manual.

Accompanying Materials

A pretest and posttest correspond to each four-page module. These can be ordered in perforated book form.

Accompanying each text is a detailed instructor's manual. Because it offers general and specific suggestions for presentation of the modules, it will not only streamline lesson planning for experienced teachers but can also serve as a training manual for new ones. It includes an Answer Key.

English Through Citizenship: A Question-and-Answer Game presents an opportunity for co-operative learning in the ESL/Civics classroom at the intermediate level. The questions and answers in this innovative game are based on the information in the federal textbooks published by the U.S. Department of Justice Immigration and Naturalization Service (1987).

For more information on accompanying materials, write or call toll free:

Delta Systems Co., Inc.
570 Rock Road Dr., Unit H
Dundee, IL 60118

1-800-323-8270
[In Illinois call (312) 551-9595]

Also to the Instructor

Did **You** **Know...**

That photocopying pages without permission is a violation of Federal Copyright law?

It deprives people of their livelihood:

The Author . . .

The Artists . . .

Been here 14 hours today. I sure hope this book sells. If it does, it will be worth it.

The Editors. . .

The Production Staff. . .

So. . . If you don't have enough material for your classes, don't make photocopies. It's not only illegal, they're more expensive.

Please buy the books you need. That's how we get paid for our work.

I'll call Delta Systems toll-free at 1-800-323-8270. They ship fast!

Module 1A: Name and Address

A Names

Please print.

Mary   Beth

first name = given name   middle name

Rivera

last name = family name

Washington

maiden name = last name before marriage
(married women only)

NAME Perez   Juan   Eduardo

last   first   middle

SIGNATURE *Juan Eduardo Perez*

B Number the names.

1 = first name   2 = middle name   3 = maiden name   4 = last name

    1   2   3   4

1. Maria Elena Hernandez de Perez

2. Ernest Robert Vargas-Gonzalez

3. Patricia Jane Jones Anderson

4. Adams-Smith, Mary Kay

5. Wong, Su-Yen

6. Washington, James P.

C Circle the last or maiden names. Underline the first or middle names.

1. (Gonzalez)

2. <u>Eduardo</u>

3. Mary-Jo

4. Smith

5. Susan Patricia

6. Williams-Jones

7. William (Bill)

8. Washington-Brown

9. Wong

10. Maria Elena

11. Mohammed

12. Green

D   Print your name.

1. NAME _____   _____   _____
        first   middle   last

2. _____   _____   _____
        (last name)   (first name)   (maiden name)

3. _____
        given name   middle name   family name

4. FULL NAME _____

E   Sign your name.

_____
signature

F   Say the names of the letters of the alphabet.

A B C D E F G H I J K L M N O P Q R S T U V W X Y Z

G   Walk around the classroom. Ask your classmates their names. Write one name on each line. Your classmates will sign if their names are correct.

	first	
	middle	
What's your	last	name, please? How do you spell it?
	maiden	
	full	

1. _____   _____
                                          signature

2   _____   _____
                                          signature

3. _____   _____
                                          signature

4. _____   _____
                                          signature

5. _____   _____
                                          signature

Addresses and Telephone Numbers

ADDRESS   <u>2270</u>   <u>Green St.</u>   <u>#205</u>
     number   street   apartment

<u>Pasadena</u>   <u>CA</u>   <u>91105</u>
city   state   zip code

TELEPHONE   <u>818</u>   <u>555-0412</u>
      area code number

St. = Street	Apt. = Apartment	CA = California
Ave. = Avenue	No. = Number	NY = New York
Blvd. = Boulevard	# = Number	TX = Texas
Rd. = Road		FL = Florida

 Circle the letters of three answers.

1. street address
    a. 515 Main Street   c. 90001   e. 2415 22nd Ave.
    b. Los Angeles CA   d. Apt. 202   f. 12000 Grand Blvd.

2. apartment number
    a. 202 First St.   c. # 101   e. Apt. No. 24
    b. Apartment 12   d. Elm Road   f. San Diego

3. city
    a. San Francisco   c. Boulevard   e. New York City
    b. California   d. Miami   f. 412 E. Oak

4. state
    a. Dallas   c. Houston   e. Florida
    b. Texas   d. No. 110   f. CA

5. zip code
    a. 91107   c. (314)   e. 312-7808
    b. 78593   d. 10027   f. 8854

6. area code
    a. 53701   c. # 333   e. (714)
    b. 998-8888   d. (213)   f. 813

7. telephone number
    a. (512)   c. 55091   e. 555-1212
    b. 993-8967   d. No. 7599   f. 850-4323

Write the information about you.

ADDRESS   _____   _____
           number   street   apartment

_____   _____   _____
city   state   zip code

TELEPHONE _____   _____
              (area code)   number

K **Ask two classmates their names, addresses and telephone numbers. Write the information on the lines.**

1. NAME _____
         last   first   middle

    ADDRESS   _____   _____
                  number   street   apartment

    _____   _____   _____
    city   state   zip code

    TELEPHONE _____   _____
               (area code)   number

2. NAME _____
         last   first   middle

    ADDRESS   _____   _____
                  number   street   apartment

    _____   _____   _____
    city   state   zip code

    TELEPHONE _____   _____
               (area code)   number

Module 1B: Biographic and Other Information

A   Vocabulary

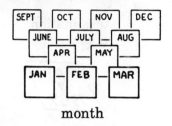   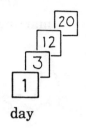   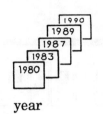   January 12, 1988
Jan. 12, 1988
1/12/88

month   day   year   date

B   Number the months in order 1–12. Then write the abbreviations.

1	2	3	4	5	6
Jan.	Feb.	Mar.	Apr.	May	June

7	8	9	10	11	12
July	Aug.	Sept.	Oct.	Nov.	Dec.

_8_ August __Aug._____   ___ January _____

___ July_____   ___ October _____

___ March_____   ___ December _____

___ April_____   ___ February _____

___ May _____   ___ June_____

___ September_____   ___ November_____

C   Match the dates. Draw lines.

1. January 24, 1956   Oct. 12, 1988
2. April 16, 1940   Dec. 25, 1968
3. October 12, 1988   1/24/56
4. February 1, 1917   7/18/90
5. December 25, 1968   3/7/77
6. March 7, 1977   11/30/39
7. November 30, 1939   4/16/40
8. July 18, 1990   2/1/17

D Vocabulary

birth

entry

marriage

termination
of marriage

application
for amnesty
or citizenship

residence
(address)

employment
(occupation)

the date today
(present time)

E Write the information and dates for you, if any.

1. Date of Birth: _____
   Month   Day   Year

2. Date of Entry into United States: _____
   month / day / year

3. Date of Marriage: _____

4. Date of Termination of Marriage: _____

5. Date of Application for Amnesty or Citizenship: _____

6. Residences Last Five Years. Present Address First.

STREET AND NUMBER	CITY	STATE	COUNTRY	FROM MONTH YEAR	TO MONTH YEAR

7. Employment Last Five Years. Present Employment First.

NAME AND ADDRESS OF EMPLOYER	OCCUPATION	FROM MONTH YEAR	TO MONTH YEAR

8. Signature _____ Date _____

F Vocabulary

passport

alien registration
number

social security
number

G Walk around the classroom. Ask your classmates their names and numbers, if any. Write the information in the boxes.

1. name

2. passport
   number

3. alien registration
   number

4. social security
   number

H Vocabulary

sex

marital status

male   female

married   single   divorced   widowed

place of birth

nationality

Monterey, Mexico
Managua, Nicaragua

Mexican

Nicaraguan

Read and circle the correct words.

NAME   LOPEZ   ANGELA   MARIA
         LAST   First   Middle

SEX   ☐ Male   ☒ Female

MARITAL STATUS   ☐ Married   ☒ Single   ☐ Divorced   ☐ Widowed

PLACE OF BIRTH   GUADALAJARA   JALISCO   MEXICO
                      city   state   country

NATIONALITY   GUATAMALAN

1. Angela's last name is | Maria.
                          | (Lopez.)

2. Angela is a | man, | and she is | married | now.
             | woman, | | not married |

3. Her country of birth is | Mexico, | but she is | Mexican.
                    | Guatemala, | | Guatemalan.

J Write the information about you.

NAME _____
         LAST   First   Middle

SEX   ☐ Male   ☐ Female

MARITAL STATUS   ☐ Married   ☐ Single   ☐ Divorced   ☐ Widowed

PLACE OF BIRTH _____
                      city   state   country

NATIONALITY _____

K Ask a classmate questions. Tell the class his or her answers.

1. Are you | married?   2. What's your | place of birth?
          | single? | nationality?
          | divorced? | occupation?
          | widowed?

Module 1C: Family

A Vocabulary

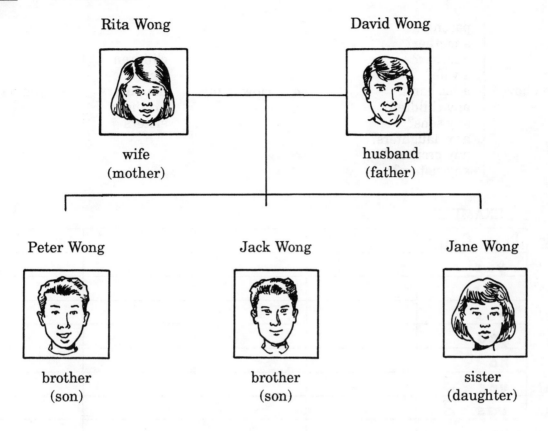

Rita Wong
wife
(mother)

David Wong
husband
(father)

Peter Wong
brother
(son)

Jack Wong
brother
(son)

Jane Wong
sister
(daughter)

parents = mother and father   children = sons and daughters

B Write words for relatives from A.

1. Rita Wong is the _____wife_____ of David Wong, and David is her _____.

2. Rita and David Wong are the _____s of Peter, Jack, and Jane Wong. Peter, Jack, and Jane are their _____.

3. Peter and Jack Wong are the _____s of Rita and David, and Jane is the _____ of Rita and David.

4. Jane Wong is the _____ of Peter and Jack, and they are her _____s.

Ask your classmates questions. Write their names, *yes* or *no*, and numbers in the boxes.

1. What's your name?

2. How do you spell it?

3. Do you have

| parents? |
| a mother? |
| a father? |
| a wife? |
| a husband? |
| any children? |
| any sons? |
| any daughters? |
| any brothers? |
| any sisters? |

4. How many

| children |
| sons |
| daughters |
| brothers |
| sisters |

do you have?

EXAMPLE

name?	Juan Cruz			
parents?	yes			
mother?	yes			
father?	yes			
wife?	yes			
husband?	no			
children?	yes 3			
sons?	yes 3			
daughters?	no			
brothers?	no			
sisters?	yes 2			

D Vocabulary

relationship   residence   applying   applicant
(relatives)

E An INS Application

You can apply for temporary or permanent residence at the INS (the Immigration and Naturalization Service). Many applications ask for information about your family.

Name	Relationship	Place of Birth	Date of Birth	Country of Residence	Applying With You?	
Rita Wong	Wife	Hong Kong	6-12-38	U. S.	☑ Yes	☐ No
Peter Wong	Son	Hong Kong	4-21-60	Hong Kong	☐ Yes	☑ No
Jack Wong	Son	U. S.	12-2-77	U. S.	☐ Yes	☑ No
Jane Wong	Daughter	U. S.	12-19-71	U. S.	☐ Yes	☑ No
Chaio Lin Wong	Brother	Korea	9-30-34	Korea	☐ Yes	☑ No
Shieh Lu	Sister	Korea	7-19-42	Hong Kong	☐ Yes	☑ No
					☐ Yes	☐ No
					☐ Yes	☐ No
					☐ Yes	☐ No
					☐ Yes	☐ No

F Answer the questions with information from the form in E

1. Is the applicant married? (Does he have a wife?) _____ **yes** _____

2. What is his wife's name? _____

3. Where was she born? (What was her place of birth?) _____

4. When was she born? (What was her date of birth?) _____

5. Where does she live? (What is her country of residence?) _____

6. Is she applying for residence with the applicant? _____

7. Does the applicant have children? _____

8. How many sons does he have? _____ How many daughters? _____

9. Are his children applying with the applicant? _____

10. How many brothers does the applicant have? _____ Sisters? _____

11. Where was his brother born? _____ When? _____

12. Where does his sister live? _____

Write the information about your parents (mother and father), husband or wife, children (sons and daughters), and brothers and sisters.

Name	Relationship	Place of Birth	Date of Birth	Country of Residence

H **Work with a classmate. Ask him or her about relatives (father, mother, husband, wife, sons, daughters, brothers, and sisters). Write the information in the form.**

1. What's his or her name?
2. How do you spell it?
3. What's his (her) relationship to you?
4. Where was he (she) born?
5. When was he (she) born?
6. Where does he (she) live?

Name	Relationship	Place of Birth	Date of Birth	Country of Residence

Module 1D: Employment

A Vocabulary

job (work)

bus boy

waiter
waitress

cook's helper

teacher's aide

secretary

deliveryperson
truck driver

hospital
worker

parking
attendant

salesclerk

sewing machine
operator

gardener

restaurant

school

office

store

factory

B **Ask your classmates the questions. Write their names and answers in the boxes.**

What's your name? (How do you spell it?)	What do you do? (What's your job?)	Where do you work?
Jorge Rios	musician	restaurant

Many application forms ask for information about your job.

8. Profession or occupation and years held
factory worker — 4 years

9. Social Security Number	10. Alien Registration Number (if any)
495-81-7666	A978654

11. Name and address of present employer (Name)
Ace Carpet Company   Ann Lee
(Number and Street)
610B Shag Ave.
(Town or City)   (State/Country)   (ZIP/Postal Code)
Los Angeles   CA   90046

12. Date employee began present employment
6/12/86

profession or occupation = job

present employer = boss now

employee = worker

employment = job

D **Circle the words.**

1. His job is | salesclerk.
   (factory worker.)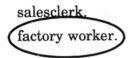

2. Last year he was a | parking attendant.
   factory worker.

3. His social security number is | 495-81-7666.
   A978654.

4. His | employer | now is | Ann Lee | at | the Go-Inn Restaurant.
   employee | | Pat Chen | | the Ace Carpet Company.

5. He began his present job on | June 12, 1986.
   December 6, 1968.

E **Write the information about your job.**

8. Profession or occupation and years held

9. Social Security Number	10. Alien Registration Number (if any)

11. Name and address of present employer (Name)
(Number and Street)
(Town or City)   (State/Country)   (ZIP/Postal Code)

12. Date employee began present employment

Ask a classmate the questions. Write the information on the form.

8. What do you do?
    How many years?

9. What's your social
    security number?

10. Do you have an
    alien registration
    number? What is it?

11. Who's your employer?
    Where do you work?
    What's the address?

12. When did you begin this
    job?

---

8. Profession or occupation and years held

_____

9. Social Security Number   **10. Alien Registration Number** (if any)

_____

11. Name and address of present employer (Name)

_____

(Number and Street)

_____

(Town or City)   (State/Country)   (ZIP/Postal Code)

_____

12. Date employee began present employment

G **The Immigration Reform and Control Act (IRCA)**

Because of the Immigration Reform and Control Act (IRCA) of 1986, all new employees must show employers some papers. These papers can be a U.S. passport, a certificate of naturalization, an alien registration card with a photograph, a social security card, or another kind of identification. The papers prove eligibility to work. The employee and the employer must fill out the I-9 Form.

If you are eligible to work, employers cannot refuse to give you a job because you are from another country.

H **Circle all the correct answers.**

1. What is IRCA?   (The Immigration Reform and Control Act.)
                          A law about the President and Congress.

2. What can new employees show employers to prove eligibility to work?

    a passport   a checkbook   a certificate of naturalization
    photographs   an English test   another kind of identification

3. What must the employee and the employer fill out?

    a social security card   an I-9 Form   a housing application

4. If you are eligible to work, can an employer refuse to give you a job because you are from another country?

                          yes   no

Module 1E:	Entry, Admission, and Establishment of Residency

A Vocabulary

temporary
resident card

application
apply

permanent
resident card

high school
college

take a
test

pass a test

study

take a course

citizenship

certificate

B How can you (or a friend or relative) become a legal permanent resident of the United States? Answer each question. Then read the information.

1. When did you become a temporary resident of the United States?
   _____: You can apply for permanent residence eighteen
   (date)   months after this date.

2. Did you go to high school or college in the United States for one year or more?
   yes = You don't have to take a test or go back to school.
   no = Go to Question 3.

3. Do you want to take the U.S. citizenship test?
   yes = If you pass, you don't have to go to school.
   no = Go to Question 4.

4. Do you want to take the "proficiency test for legalization?"
   yes = If you pass, you don't have to go to school.
   no = Go to Question 5.

5. Did you study or are you studying English and citizenship for the required number of hours in an INS-approved course?
   yes = Get a "certificate of satisfactory pursuit" or certificate of completion from your school.
   no = Take an INS-approved course.

C Circle the answers to the questions about the card.

1. What kind of card is it?
   (temporary resident)
   permanent resident

2. What is the resident identification number
   on the card?
   12/28/89
   A77880321

3. When did Angela become a temporary U.S. resident?   on June 28, 1987
   on January 24, 1959

4. How old is Angela?   under twenty years old
   over thirty years old

5. After what date can Angela apply for permanent residence?   June 28, 1987
   December 28, 1988

6. When does the card expire (become no good)?   December 28, 1987
   December 28, 1989

D Circle the words.

1. Temporary U.S. residents can apply for | permanent residence |
   | U.S. citizenship |

   eighteen months after the | issue | date of their temporary resident card.
   | expiration |

2. If they went to | an INS school, | they don't have to
   | a U.S. high school or college, |

   | take a citizenship or proficiency test.
   | apply for permanent residence.

3. If they didn't go to school or take and pass a test, they can take a course in

   | legalization interviews.
   | English and citizenship.

4. They can get a | "certificate of satisfactory pursuit" | from
   | high school diploma |

   | a lawyer's | school.
   | an INS-approved |

E   Vocabulary

form   fees   documents   photograph   interview
              fee receipt   appointment

F   Steps to Permanent Residence

   Do you have INS Form I-698? You can get it from the INS.

   Fill out the form. Send it to the INS with the necessary fees and documents and one photograph.

   Wait for your fee receipt and interview appointment.

   Go to the interview. Get proof of permanent residence at the interview.

   The INS will send your permanent resident card ("green card").

G   Match the sentence parts. Draw lines.

1. You can get Form I-698   at the INS interview.
2. Fill out   Form I-698.
3. Send the form to the INS   your fee receipt and interview appointment.
4. Wait for   your green card.
5. Get your proof of permanent residence   with fees, documents, and one photograph.
6. The INS will send   from the INS.

H   ## Number the sentences in correct time order.

| 1 | 2 | 3 | 4 |

___ Get Form I-698 from the INS.

_2_ Take a test or an INS-approved course in English and citizenship.

_1_ Become a temporary resident of the United States.

___ Apply for permanent residence eighteen months or more after the issue date on your temporary resident card.

| 5 | 6 | 7 | 8 |

___ Wait for your fee receipt and interview appointment with the INS.

___ Now you are a permanent resident with the green card.

___ Send the form with the fee, documents, and your photograph to the INS.

___ Get proof of permanent residence at the INS interview.

I   ## How does a temporary resident become a permanent resident? Tell the steps from the pictures.

* The information in this module is from *The Path to Permanent Residence / La Senda a la Residencia Permanente*, a booklet published by the U.S. Department of Justice, Immigration and Naturalization Service.

Symbols and Holidays

Module 2A: American Symbols

A Vocabulary

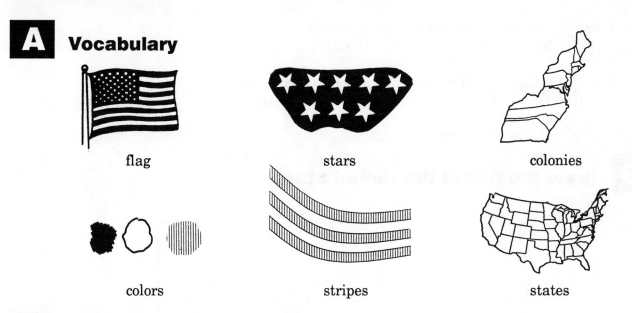

flag stars colonies

colors stripes states

B The Flag of the United States

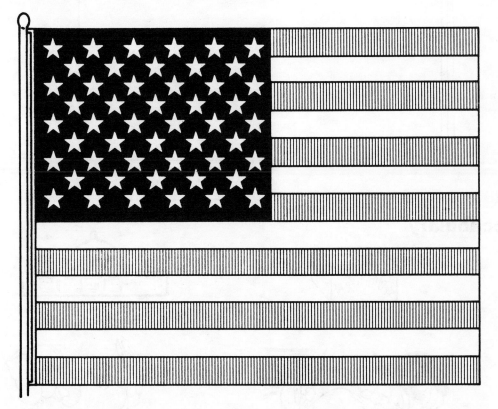

The colors of the flag are red, white, and blue. It has thirteen stripes. The stripes are symbols for the thirteen colonies. It has fifty stars. The stars are symbols for the fifty states.

C   Circle the words.

1. The |(colors)| of the flag of the United States are red, white, and | black.
    | stars | | blue.

2. It has | thirteen | stripes for the | colonies.
    | fifty | | states.

3. The | thirteen | stars are symbols for the | colonies.
    | fifty | | states.

D   Draw the flag of the United States.

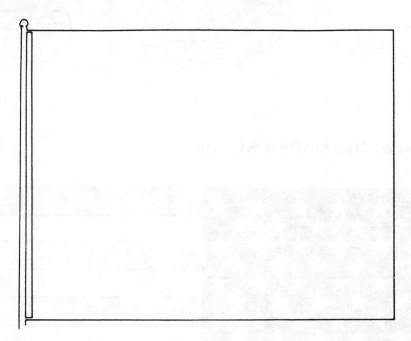

E   Vocabulary

freedom

the government

the Revolution

political parties
(Republicans and Democrats)

More American Symbols

    The Liberty Bell is the symbol of the American Revolution.

   The Statue of Liberty is the symbol of the land of freedom.

    Uncle Sam is the symbol of the U.S. government.

    The donkey is the symbol of the Democratic Party.

    The elephant is the symbol of the Republican Party.

G Circle the words.

1. The | Liberty Bell
        | Statue of Liberty | is the symbol of the American Revolution.

2. The | elephant
        | Statue of Liberty | is the symbol of the land of freedom.

3. Uncle Sam is the symbol of the U.S. | Revolution.
                                        | government.

4. The donkey is the symbol of the | Democratic
                                    | Republican | Party.

5. The | donkey
       | elephant | is the symbol of the Republican Party.

H   Write the letters of the words in the crossword puzzle.

ACROSS

1. _____ states

3.

6. the _____ party

7. _____ Sam

DOWN

1.

2. The Statue of _____

4.

5.

Module 2B: Thanksgiving and Independence Day

A Vocabulary

Pilgrims   ship   winter   spring   Indians

the land   fall   dinner   give thanks   turkey

B Thanksgiving Day

Thanksgiving Day is the fourth Thursday in November. In 1620 the Pilgrims came to America on a ship. They had a difficult first winter. In the spring the Indians helped the Pilgrims. They learned about the land. In the fall they gave thanks at a big dinner. It was the first Thanksgiving. Now American families and friends give thanks at a big dinner every Thanksgiving. They eat turkey.

C Circle the words.

1. Thanksgiving   Day is the fourth Thursday in   January.
   Independence   November.

2. It began with the   Pilgrims.
                        colonies.

3. They had a difficult first   summer.
                                 winter.

4. They learned about the land from the   English.
                                           Indians.

5. In the fall they   gave thanks   at a big dinner.
                       had fireworks

D Vocabulary

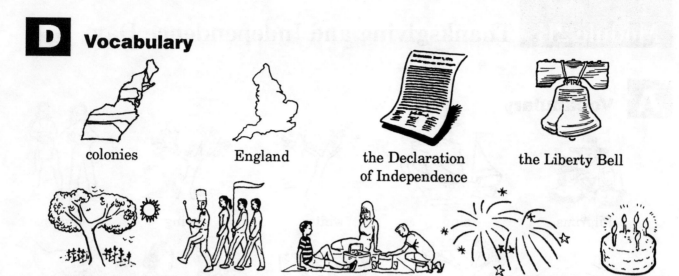

colonies   England   the Declaration   the Liberty Bell
                                   of Independence

summer   parade   picnic   fireworks   birthday

E American Independence Day

The Fourth of July is American Independence Day. On July 4, 1776, people from the thirteen American colonies signed the Declaration of Independence from England. The Liberty Bell rang. Now every summer Americans have parades, picnics, and fireworks on the Fourth of July. It is the birthday of the United States.

F Circle the words.

1. The | First of January | is American | Flag | Day.
      | Fourth of July | | Independence |

2. On July 4, | 1492, | people from the thirteen American | colonies | signed the
            | 1776, | | states |
   | Revolution.
   | Declaration of Independence.

3. The | Statue of Liberty | rang.
      | Liberty Bell |

4. Now Americans have | parades, | colors, | and | stars | on the Fourth of July.
                     | stripes | picnics, | | fireworks |

5. It is the birthday of | the United States.
                        | England.

G   Write T for Thanksgiving Day. Write I for Independence Day.

1. __T__   It's the fourth Thursday in November.
2. ___   It's in the summer.
3. ___   It began in 1621.
4. ___   It began in 1776.
5. ___   It began with the Pilgrims.
6. ___   It began with the Declaration of Independence.
7. ___   The Liberty Bell rang.
8. ___   The Pilgrims had a big dinner with the Indians.
9. ___   Americans have parades and fireworks.
10. ___   Americans give thanks at a turkey dinner.

Circle the words in the puzzle. Write the words on the lines.

```
P I L G R I M S P R I N G D P A R A D E
E F A L L F G H T U R K E Y I J K L M N
S H I P O P F I R E W O R K S Q B A Z Y
T H A N K S G I V I N G R S U M M E R X
U W I N T E R V P I C N I C W X L A N D
T S R Q L I B E R T Y P B E L L O N M L
G I N D E P E N D E N C E H D A Y I J K
I N D I A N F E D B I R T H D A Y C B A
```

summer

Module 2C: More National Holidays

A Read the sentences. Circle the eleven dates on the calendar.

1. Martin Luther King, Jr.'s birthday is on January 15. Martin Luther King, Jr. Day is the third Monday in January.

2. President Abraham Lincoln's birthday is February 12, and George Washington's birthday is February 22. Presidents Day is the third Monday in February.

3. Memorial Day is May 30 or the last Monday in May.

4. Labor Day is the first Monday in September.

5. Columbus Day is October 12 or the second Monday in October.

6. Veterans Day is November 11.

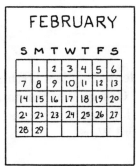

B Finish this sentence in many ways.

EXAMPLE: Martin Luther King, Jr.'s birthday is on January 15.

_____ is on _____.
(day or holiday)   (date)

C   Vocabulary

celebration

civil rights leader

in honor of

integration

D   Some Famous Birthdays

Martin Luther King, Jr. Day is in honor of a famous civil rights leader. Martin Luther King, Jr. believed in integration and wanted to help black people.

Presidents Day is a birthday celebration for two famous Presidents. George Washington was the first President of the United States. Abraham Lincoln was President at the time of the Civil War.

E   Circle the words.

1. Martin Luther King, Jr. was a famous | military
    civil rights | leader.

2. He believed in | slavery
    integration | and wanted to help | black people.
    students.

3. Presidents Day is a | birthday
    picnic | celebration in honor of

    George Washington
    Christopher Columbus | and | the Pilgrims.
    Abraham Lincoln.

4. Washington was the | first
    third | President of the United States.

5. Lincoln was President at the time of the | Revolutionary
    Civil | War.

F Vocabulary

patriotic

the Civil War

World War II

soldiers

flowers

graves

the weekend

vacation

G Some Patriotic Holidays

Memorial Day began after the Civil War. Veterans Day began after World War II. On these patriotic days Americans remember the soldiers of all American wars. They put flags and flowers on their graves.

Labor Day is part of the last weekend of summer vacation. It is a celebration in honor of work and workers. After Labor Day, students go back to school.

Columbus Day is a holiday in honor of Christopher Columbus. Columbus discovered America on October 12, 1492. School children learn about Columbus for this patriotic day.

H Write the letters on the lines.

M = Memorial Day   C = Columbus Day
L = Labor Day   V = Veterans Day

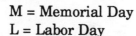

1. **L** It's part of the last weekend of summer vacation.
2. ___ It began after the Civil War.
3. ___ It began after World War I.
4. ___ It's a holiday in honor of Christopher Columbus.
5. ___ ___ On these days patriotic people remember the soldiers of American wars.
6   ___ It's a holiday in honor of work and workers.
7   ___ ___ On these days Americans put flags and flowers on graves.
8. ___ After this holiday, students go back to school.
9. ___ On this day in 1492, Columbus discovered America.
10. ___ School children learn about Columbus for this patriotic day.

  Do you know facts about other American holidays? Tell the class.

Americans

Module 3A: Famous Presidents

A Vocabulary

the Revolutionary War

farmer

military leader

signer

elected

President

birthday

national holiday

B George Washington

Before the Revolutionary War, George Washington was a farmer in the colony of Virginia. He was the military leader of the colonists in the war and a signer of the Declaration of Independence. After the war, people from the thirteen American states elected Washington President of the new country. He was the first President of the United States. George Washington was "the father of our country."

C Circle the words.

Before the | (Revolutionary) / Civil | War, George Washington was a

| president / farmer | in Virginia. He was the military | slave / leader | of the

colonists in the war and a | writer / signer | of the Declaration of

Independence. He was the | first / third | President of the United States.

George Washington was | "the father of our country." / "Uncle Sam."

D   Vocabulary

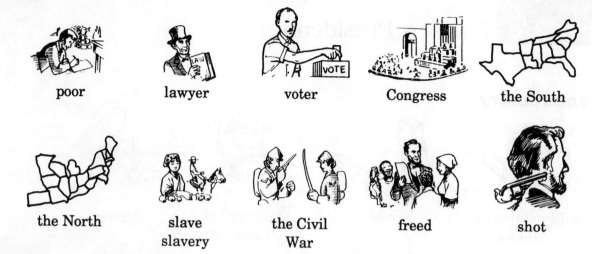

poor   lawyer   voter   Congress   the South

the North   slave   the Civil   freed   shot
                   slavery   War

E   Abraham Lincoln

The family of Abraham Lincoln was poor, and he didn't go to school. But he studied and became a lawyer. Voters in Illinois elected him to Congress. In 1860 voters of the United States elected him President. At that time farmers in the South had slaves. Many people in the North were against slavery, and the Civil War started. Lincoln freed the slaves with the Emancipation Proclamation. In 1865 John Wilkes Booth shot President Lincoln.

F   Match the sentence parts. Draw lines.

1. The Lincoln family   elected him to Congress.

2. Lincoln studied and   had slaves.

3. Voters in Illinois   was poor.

4. Voters of the U.S.   were against slavery.

5. Farmers in the South   shot President Lincoln.

6. People in the North   became a lawyer.

7. With the Emancipation Proclamation, Lincoln   freed the slaves.

8. John Wilkes Booth   elected him President.

G Vocabulary

Martin Luther
King, Jr.

civil rights

education

medical
care

Communism

Africa

Asia

the moon

H John F. Kennedy

The voters of the United States elected John F. Kennedy President in 1960. Kennedy liked the ideas of Martin Luther King, Jr. He believed in civil rights and wanted to help black people and poor people. He asked Congress for money for education and medical care. Kennedy was against Communism. He wanted to help the poor countries of Africa, Asia, and South America. He also wanted to send a man to the moon. But on November 22, 1963, Lee Harvey Oswald shot President Kennedy.

I Write the words from the box on the lines.

Communism	medical care	Martin Luther King, Jr.	shot
education	civil rights	poor and black	moon

John F. Kennedy became President in 1961. Kennedy liked the ideas of _Martin Luther King, Jr._.

He believed in _____ and wanted to help _____ people in the

United States. He asked Congress for more money for _____ and _____.

Kennedy was against _____. He wanted to send a man to the _____. But in 1963

Lee Harvey Oswald _____ President Kennedy.

Write W for George Washington. Write L for Abraham Lincoln. Write K for John F. Kennedy.

1789-1796   1861-1865   1961-1963

1. **L**   His family was poor, but he studied and became a lawyer.

2. ___   He believed in civil rights for black people and wanted to help poor people.

3. ___   He was a farmer in Virginia before the Revolutionary War and a military leader in the war.

4. ___   He was against Communism and wanted to help poor countries.

5. ___   He signed the Declaration of Independence.

6. ___   He was a Congressman from Illinois, and he became President in 1861.

7. ___   He was "the father of our country."

8. ___   He was against slavery, and he freed the slaves with the Emancipation Proclamation.

9. ___   He wanted to send a man to the moon, but Lee Harvey Oswald shot him.

 Do you know facts about other Presidents of the United States? Tell the class.

Module 3B: The History of Immigration

A Vocabulary

immigrants
immigrate
immigration

the American
Revolution

colonies

Protestants

settled

California and
the Southwest

slaves

factories

Catholics

discrimination

Jewish people

the New World

railroad

mine

passed laws

official

Ellis Island

handicapped

farms

World War II

B Immigration to the United States

The first immigrants to America were mostly from Europe. Before the American Revolution, the thirteen colonies were British. Most of the people were Protestants. The Spanish settled in the Southwest. Black Africans came to the United States as slaves.

Then many European immigrants arrived to work in factories. Poor Irish Catholics left Ireland because there was discrimination against them in their country. Catholics, Protestants, and Jewish people came to the New World from Germany.

Chinese immigrants came to work on the railroads and the mines of California and the Southwest. There was discrimination against them in this country. Then the U.S. government passed laws against Asian immigration.

More and more Europeans immigrated to America from almost every country in Europe. They saw the Statue of Liberty from their ships. If they were poor, most of them had to stop at Ellis Island in New York. Many times, immigration officials sent sick or handicapped people back to their countries.

North and South Americans began to immigrate to the United States. Many Mexicans and Central Americans still work on the farms and in the cities of California and Texas. After World War II, more and more Asians came to this country.

the 1600's | the 1700's | 1820 to 1880 | 1850 to 1870 | 1880 to 1930 | the 1900's

C Finish these sentences in different ways.

EXAMPLE: In the 1600s many Europeans came to the United States. = In the 1600s many people from Europe immigrated to the United States.

In the _____, | many | _____s
(years) | | (nationality)

Between _____ and _____, | | people from _____
(year)   (year) | | (country)

came | to the United States.
immigrated |

D Match the sentence parts. Draw lines.

1. The first immigrants were   British.

2. The thirteen colonies were   Spanish.

3. Many settlers in the Southwest were   black Africans

4. The slaves in the United States were   mostly European and Protestant.

5. Many Irish immigrants were   Protestant, Catholic, and Jewish.

6. German immigrants were   poor and Catholic.

7. The railroad and mine workers of   Asian.
   California and the Southwest were

8. Many farm and city workers in California   Chinese.
   and Texas were or are

9. Many immigrants after World World II   Mexican or Central American.
   were

E Circle the words.

1. Between 1880 and 1930, many | European / South American | immigrants came
to this country to work in the | schools. / factories.

2. Many poor Irish people left their country because there was
| abolition / discrimination | against | Catholics. / Jewish people.

3. In the 1860s, Chinese immigrants often worked | on the railroads / in restaurants
and in the | colonies. / mines.

4. The U.S. government passed laws against | immigration. / revolutions.

5. Immigration officials at | the Statue of Liberty / Ellis Island | often sent
| sick or handicapped / Protestant | people back to their countries.

F Answer the questions.

1. When did immigrants from your native country first come to the United States?
(EXAMPLES: in the 1600s, between 1800 and 1860, before World World I)

2. Why did they come? (EXAMPLES: for religious reasons, to find work, to have a better life)

3. How did they come? (EXAMPLES: by ship, on foot)

4. Where did they arrive? (EXAMPLES: at Ellis Island, in San Francisco)

5. Where did many of them work? (EXAMPLES: in the factories, on farms)

6. Why did some of them have to go back to their country? (EXAMPLES: because they were
sick, because they were illegal)

Module 3C: Historical Figures

A Vocabulary

printed

invented

the Postal Service

the right to vote

the Red Cross

victims

natural disaster

light bulb

movie projector

phonograph

B Some Famous Americans

1706 - 1790

Benjamin Franklin wrote and printed books and newspapers. He invented things. He helped write the Declaration of Independence and the U.S. Constitution. He was a high official of the U.S. Postal Service and represented the United States in other countries.

1820 -1906

Susan B. Anthony was a famous leader in the fight for women's rights. She helped win the right to vote for women.

1821 -1912

Clara Barton began the American Red Cross. She helped the victims of wars and natural disasters.

1847 -1937

Thomas A. Edison invented many things. Some of his inventions were the light bulb, the movie projector, and the phonograph.

C Circle the words.

1. Benjamin Franklin wrote, printed | (books and newspapers,) movie programs,

and | manufactured invented | things. He helped write the Declaration of Independence and the

| U.S. Constitution. the Emancipation Proclamation. | He was a high official of | Congress the U.S. Postal Service

and | represented worked against | the United States in other countries.

2. Martin Luther King Susan B. Anthony | fought for | women's rights. slavery. | She helped win the right to

| work in factories vote | for women.

3. Clara Barton began | the American Red Cross. the United Farm Workers. | She helped the victims of

| integration. wars and natural disasters.

4. Thomas A. Edison invented the | light bulb, automobile, | the | computer phonograph,

and the | printing press. movie projector.

D Vocabulary

factory

manufactured (assembly line)

the United Nations

jazz (music)

band

union

farm workers

grape and lettuce fields

E More Famous Americans

Henry Ford changed factory work in the United States. He manufactured cars on the assembly line.

1863 - 1947

Eleanor Roosevelt was the wife of President Franklin D. Roosevelt. She fought for equal rights for people of all countries and worked with the United Nations.

1884 - 1962

Duke Ellington wrote music and led big bands. He was famous for his jazz.

1899 - 1974

Cesar Chavez leads the union of the UFW (United Farm Workers). He helps workers in the grape and lettuce fields.

1927 -

F Write the words from the box on the lines.

wife	grape	factory	the assembly line	equal rights
jazz	lettuce	big bands	the United Nations	the UFW

1. Henry Ford changed __**factory**__ work in the United States. He manufactured cars on

    _____.

2. Eleanor Roosevelt was the _____ of President Franklin D. Roosevelt. She fought for

    _____ for people of all countries and worked with _____.

3. Duke Ellingon wrote _____ and other music and led _____.

4. Cesar Chavez leads _____. He helps farm workers in the _____ and

    _____ fields.

G   **Number these people 1–8 in correct time order (the time of their birth).**

___ Eleanor Roosevelt   ___ Susan B. Anthony

___ Henry Ford   ___ Cesar Chavez

___ Clara Barton   ___ Duke Ellington

_1_ Benjamin Franklin   ___ Thomas A. Edison

H   **Make eight sentences with this pattern. Use the information from the pictures on pages 41 and 43.**

EXAMPLE: Benjamin Franklin lived from 1706 to 1790.

_____ lived from _____ to _____.
(name)   (year)   (year)

I   **These sentences are about the people in G. Write their names on the lines.**

1. _Eleanor Roosevelt_ was the wife of a President, fought for equal rights for people of all countries, and worked with the United Nations.

2. _____ fought for women's rights and helped win the right to vote for women.

3. _____ changed factory work with his car assembly line.

4. _____ helped victims of wars and natural disasters with the American Red Cross.

5. _____ was famous for his jazz and big bands.

6. _____ helps the workers in the fields with his union (the UFW).

7. _____ was a writer, printer, high official, and government representative. He helped write some famous documents.

8. _____ invented the light bulb, the movie projector, and the phonograph.

J   **Do you know other facts about these eight people or other famous Americans? Tell the class.**

Module 4A: The Geography of the United States

A VOCABULARY

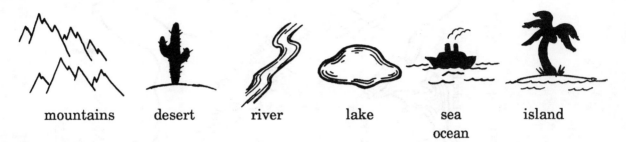

| mountains | desert | river | lake | sea ocean | island |

B Look at the map on the next page. Circle the words.

1. Canada, the United States, and Mexico are | states.
   countries.

2. The Atlantic and the Pacific are | lakes.
   oceans.

3. The Mississippi and the Missouri are | mountains.
   rivers.

4. The Mojave is | a desert.
   an island.

5. The Appalachian Mountains are in the | eastern | part of the United States.
   western

6. Lake Superior and Lake Huron are in the | northern | part of the United States.
   southern

7. The Mississippi River is in the | middle | of the United States.
   gulf

8. There are | deserts | in the Atlantic Ocean.
   islands

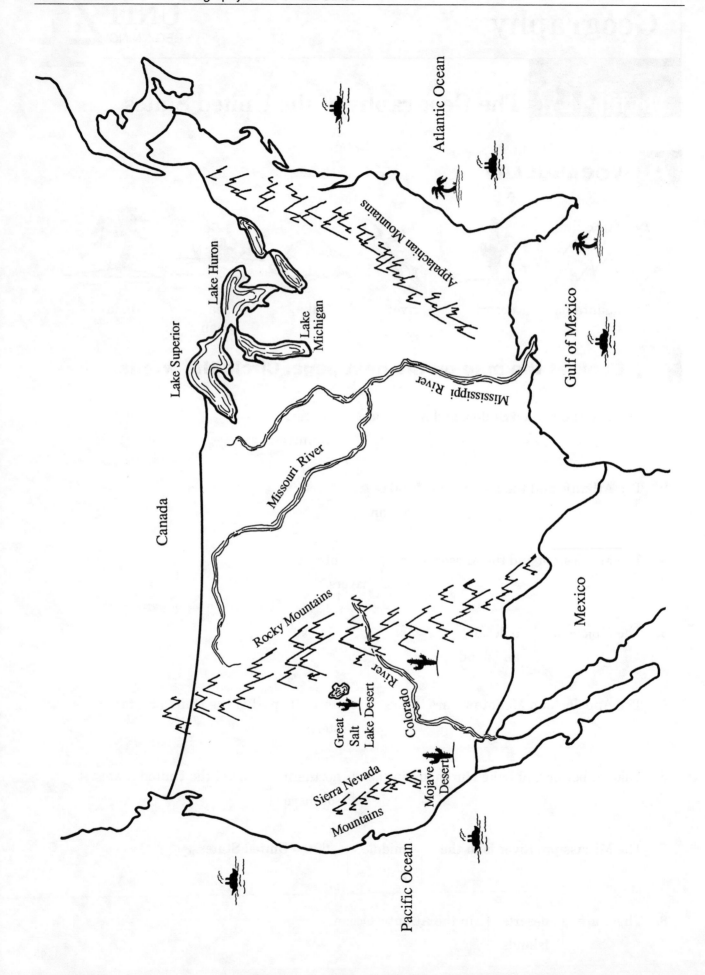

C Write the words from the boxes.

north	south	east	west

1. Canada is ____north____ of the United States.
2. The Gulf of Mexico is _____ of the United States.
3. The Atlantic Ocean is _____ of the United States.
4. The Pacific Ocean is _____ of the United States.

northern	southern	eastern	western	middle

5. The Appalachian Mountains are in the _____ part of the United States.
6. Lake Superior is in the _____ part of the United States.
7. The Mississippi River is in the _____ of the United States.
8. There are deserts in the _____ and _____ parts of the United States.

D Write names from the map.

countries

Canada _____

_____

_____

mountains

_____

_____

_____

deserts

_____

_____

rivers

_____

_____

_____

lakes

_____

_____

_____

oceans / gulf

_____

_____

E Write the letters from the map on the lines.

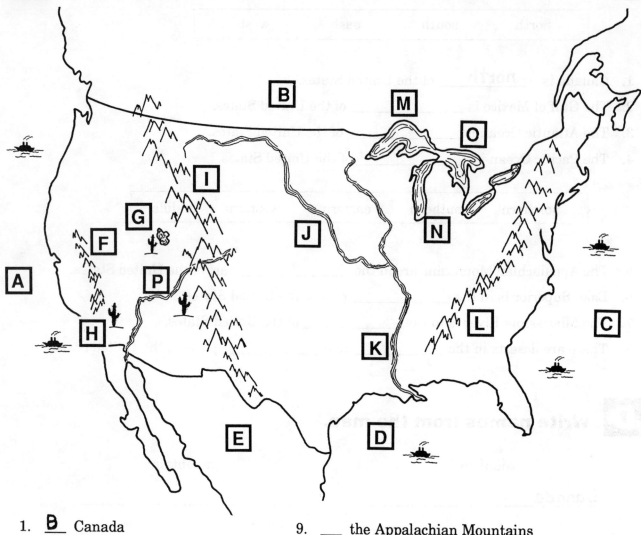

1. **B** Canada

2. ___ Mexico

3. ___ the Atlantic Ocean

4. ___ the Pacific Ocean

5. ___ the Gulf of Mexico

6. ___ the Mississippi River

7. ___ the Missouri River

8. ___ the Colorado River

9. ___ the Appalachian Mountains

10. ___ the Rocky Mountains

11. ___ the Sierra Nevada Mountains

12. ___ Lake Superior

13. ___ Lake Michigan

14. ___ Lake Huron

15. ___ the Mojave Desert

16. ___ the Great Salt Lake Desert

Module 4B: Famous Places

A Vocabulary

colonies

signed

the Declaration of
Independence

the Constitution

the Liberty Bell

Congress

the President

the Civil War

cities

B Famous Government Buildings

On July 4, 1776, people from the thirteen American colonies
signed the Declaration of Independence from England in
Independence Hall. People from the thirteen states signed the
Constitution here in 1787. Independence Hall is in Philadelphia, Pennsylvania. The Liberty Bell is here.

Now the Declaration of Independence and the Constitution are
in the National Archives. The Archives are in Washington,
D.C. Washington, D.C. is the capital city of the United States.

Congress meets in the U.S. Capitol Building. It is in Washington, D.C.

The President of the United States lives in the White House. It is in Washington, D.C.

The Washington Monument is in honor of George Washington. He was the first President of the United States. The Washington Monument is in Washington, D.C.

The Lincoln Memorial is in honor of Abraham Lincoln. He was the President of the United States at the time of the Civil War. The Lincoln Memorial is in Washington, D.C.

C Match the places, things, and people. Draw lines.

1. Independence Hall   the Declaration of Independence and the U.S. Constitution now

2. the National Archives   the first President of the United States

3. the U.S. Capitol Building   the President at the time of the Civil War

4. the White House   the President of the United States now

5. the Washington Monument   the Liberty Bell

6. the Lincoln Memorial   Congress

D Circle the words.

1. On July 4, 1776, people signed the | Declaration of Independence
   | Constitution

   in | Independence Hall.
   | the Statue of Liberty.

2. The | U.S. Capital | is in Independence Hall in | Washington, D.C.
   | Liberty Bell | | Philadelphia.

3. Now the Declaration of Independence and the | Constitution
   | Lincoln Memorial

   are in | the White House | in the capital city of the United States.
   | the National Archives |

4. Congress | meets in the Capitol Building in Washington, D.C.
   The colony |

5. The President of the United States lives in | the White House.
   | New York City.

6. The Washington Monument and the Lincoln Memorial are in honor of
   | signers | of the United States.
   | Presidents |

7. George Washington | was the first President of the United States.
   Abraham Lincoln |

8. Abraham Lincoln was President at the time of | the Revolution.
   | the Civil War.

E Vocabulary

bridge   arch   canyon   faces

F Other Famous Places

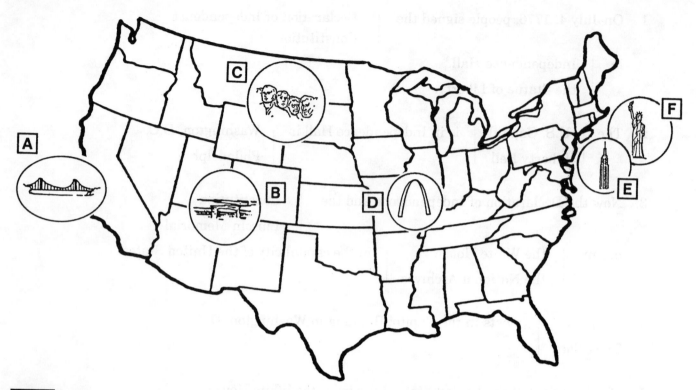

G Match the pictures from the map with these sentences. Write the letters A-F on the lines.

1. ___ The Statue of Liberty is the symbol of freedom. It is in New York.

2. ___ The Empire State Building is a very tall building in New York City.

3. ___ The Gateway Arch is the gateway to the West. It is on the Mississippi River in St. Louis, Missouri.

4. ___ The Grand Canyon of the Colorado River is in Arizona.

5. ___ Mount Rushmore shows the faces of four famous Presidents of the United States. The Presidents are George Washington, Thomas Jefferson, Theodore Roosevelt, and Abraham Lincoln. Mt. Rushmore is in South Dakota.

6. ___ You can cross San Francisco Bay on the Golden Gate Bridge.

H Tell about the places in the map in F.

Module 4C: States and Cities: The West

A Vocabulary

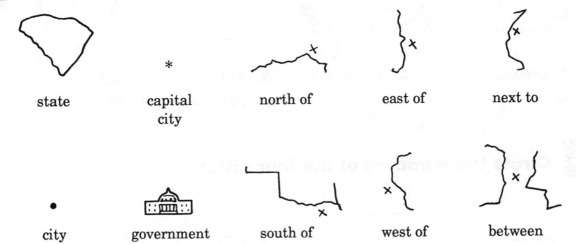

state   capital city   north of   east of   next to

city   government   south of   west of   between

B The States and Cities of the United States

Circle the numbers of the four states.

(1.) Nebraska   3. Kansas City   5. El Paso   7. California
2. Omaha   4. Texas   6. New Mexico   8. Reno

 Circle the numbers of the four cities.

1. Seattle   3. Arizona   5. Denver   7. Salt Lake City
2. Utah   4. Las Vegas   6. Idaho   8. Wyoming

 Circle the numbers of the four capital cities (state government).

1. Phoenix   3. Albuquerque   5. Honolulu   7. Montana
2. Cheyenne   4. Salem   6. Alaska   8. Juneau

 Match the cities and states. Draw lines.

1. Kansas City   Alaska
2. Tucson   California
3. San Diego   Arizona
4. Anchorage   Kansas

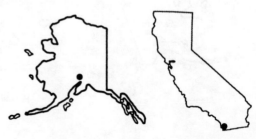

G Match the capital cities and the states. Draw lines.

1. Bismarck   South Dakota

2. Pierre   North Dakota

3. Boise   Oklahoma

4. Oklahoma City   Idaho

H Circle the words.

1. Tulsa and Dallas are | cities.
                        | states.

2. Fort Worth | and | Seattle | are states.
   Texas | | Washington |

3. Albuquerque | is a city in New Mexico.
   Las Vegas |

4. Los Angeles | and | El Paso | are cities in California.
   Phoenix | | San Francisco |

5. The state government is in the | capital city | of every state.
                                  | middle |

6. Boise is the capital city of | Idaho.
                                | Arizona.

7. Houston | is the capital of Texas.
   Austin |

8. Montana is | north | of Idaho and Wyoming.
              | south |

9. Kansas is south of | Nebraska | and east of | Missouri.
                      | Nevada | | Colorado.

10. Idaho is | west of | Oregon and | north of | Nevada and Utah.
             | next to | | between |

I Write the letters of the states from the map.

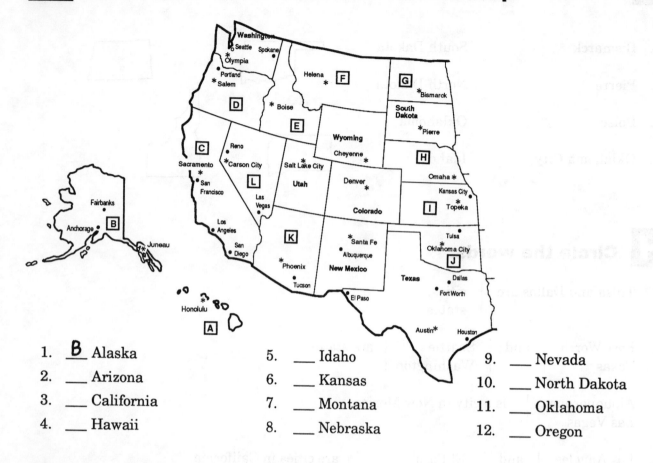

1. **B** Alaska
2. ___ Arizona
3. ___ California
4. ___ Hawaii

5. ___ Idaho
6. ___ Kansas
7. ___ Montana
8. ___ Nebraska

9. ___ Nevada
10. ___ North Dakota
11. ___ Oklahoma
12. ___ Oregon

J Finish these sentences in many ways.

1. _____ is a city in the state of _____ .

2. _____ is the capital city of _____ .

3. _____ is | north | of _____ .
                        | south |
                        | east |
                        | west |

4. _____ is next to _____ .

5. _____ is between _____ and _____ .

Module 4D: States and Cities: The East

A The States and Cities of the United States

Some Other Major Cities:

New York
New York City
Buffalo

New Jersey
Newark

Pennsylvania
Philadelphia
Pittsburgh

Maryland
Baltimore

Washington D.C.

Florida
Miami

Louisiana
New Orleans

Tennessee
Memphis

Ohio
Cincinnatti
Cleveland

Michigan
Detroit

Wisconsin
Milwaukee

Illinois
Chicago

B Circle the numbers of the four states.

1. Maine   3. Maryland   5. Newark   7. Kentucky
2. Boston   4. Atlanta   6. Florida   8. Trenton

C Circle the numbers of the four cities.

1. St.Louis   3. Wisconsin   5. Detroit   7. New Orleans
2. Michigan   4. Chicago   6. Ohio   8. Tennessee

D Circle the numbers of the four capital cities (state government).

1. New York   3. Indiana   5. Nashville   7. Milwaukee
2. Richmond   4. Hartford   6. Illinois   8. Madison

E Match the cities and states. Draw lines.

1. Boston   New York
2. New York City   Pennsylvania
3. Philadelphia   Ohio
4. Cleveland   Massachusetts

F **Match the capital cities and the states. Draw lines.**

1. St. Paul   Mississippi

2. Charleston   West Virginia

3. Tallassee   Minnesota

4. Jackson   Florida

G **Circle the words.**

1. Des Moines and Little Rock are | (cities.)
                                   | states.

2. Boston | and | Atlanta | are states.
   New Hampshire | | Georgia |

3. Chicago | is a city in Illinois.
   St. Louis |

4. Pittsburgh | and | Columbus | are cities in Ohio.
   Cincinnati | | Philadelphia |

5. The state government is in the | capital city | of every state.
                                  | middle |

6. Montgomery is the capital city of | Arkansas.
                                     | Alabama.

7. Baton Rouge | is the capital of Iowa.
   Des Moines |

8. Maine is | north | of New Hampshire and Vermont.
            | south |

9. Indiana is south of | Michigan | and east of | Pennsylvania.
                       | Missouri | | Illinois.

10. West Virginia is | south of | Delaware and | west of | Ohio and Virginia.
                     | next to | | between |

H Write the letters of the states from the map.

1. **A** Arkansas
2. ___ Connecticut
3. ___ Delaware
4. ___ Florida

5. ___ Georgia
6. ___ Indiana
7. ___ Kentucky
8. ___ Michigan

9. ___ Minnesota
10. ___ Missouri
11. ___ Mississippi
12. ___ Virginia

I Finish these sentences in many ways.

1. _____ is a city in the state of _____.

2. _____ is the capital city of _____.

3. _____ is | north | of _____.
                            | south |
                            | east |
                            | west |

4. _____ is next to _____.

5. _____ is between _____ and _____.

Citizenship

Module 5A: Becoming a Citizen

A Vocabulary

application
package

INS

biographic
information
sheet

fingerprint
chart

police
station

documents

photographs

interview
appointment

B First Steps to Citizenship

Get an application package from the Immigration and Naturalization Service (INS).

Fill out the application form, the biographic information sheet, and the fingerprint chart.

Get fingerprinted at a police station or the INS.

Send the application package with other necessary documents and three photographs of your face to the INS. Wait for an interview appointment.

C Match the sentence parts. Draw lines.

1. Get an application package — an interview appointment.

2. Fill out — at the police station or INS.

3. Get fingerprinted — other documents and three photographs.

4. Send the package to the INS with — from the INS.

5. Wait for — the form, sheet, and chart.

D Vocabulary

oral
examination

dictation
test

petition for
naturalization

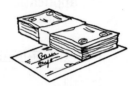

fee

court

judge

oath of
allegiance

certificate of
naturalization

E More Steps to Citizenship

Go to the interview. Answer the questions about the United States in the oral examination. Then take the dictation test.

File the petition for naturalization. Pay the fee.

Wait for the court hearing. Go to court. Talk to the judge.

Take the oath of allegiance. Get the certificate of naturalization.

F **Circle the words.**

1. Go to the | interview.
                | application.

2. Take the oral | hearing | and take the | dictation test.
                   | examination | | biographic chart.

3. Go to the | document package | and talk to the | judge
               | court hearing | | police

4. Take the | interview appointment.
              | oath of allegiance.

5. Get the | fingerprint fee.
             | certificate of naturalization.

G **Number the sentences in time order.**

1	2	3	4	5

___ Send the application package with other necessary documents and three photographs to the INS.

___ Get fingerprinted at the police station or the INS.

_1_ Get an application package from the INS.

___ Wait for an interview appointment.

_2_ Fill out the application form, the biographic information sheet, and the fingerprint chart.

6	7	8	9	10

___ File the petition for naturalization and pay the fee.

___ Take the oath of allegiance.

___ Answer the questions in the oral interview and take the dictation test.

___ Get the certificate of naturalization.

___ Talk to the judge at the court hearing.

H How do you become a citizen? Tell the steps from the pictures.

1

2

3

4

5

6

7

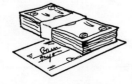

8

9

10

11

12

13

14

The U.S. Constitution

Module 6A: Overview of the Constitution

A The Constitution of the United States

After the Revolutionary War (the war of independence from England), the basis of the new American government was the Articles of Confederation. But this document did not give enough power to the national government. Representatives of twelve American states met in Philadelphia in 1787. They wrote a new government plan at this Constitutional Convention. This document was the U.S. Constitution.

The Constitution is the most important document of the United States government. It is the highest law of the land. It gives the federal (national) government powers and limits (controls) those powers. It gives rights to the people.

B Match the questions and answers. Draw lines.

1. What were the Articles of Confederation?

    They wrote the Constitution of the United States.

2. Why did the representatives of the thirteen new American states meet in Philadelphia in 1787?

    They were the plan for the new American government after the Revolutionary War.

3. What did these representatives do at the Constitutional Convention?

    It gives the government powers and limits those powers.

4. What is the U.S. Constitution?

    Because the Articles of Confederation didn't give the national government enough power.

5. How is the Constitution a plan for the federal government?

    It gives the people rights and freedoms.

6. What does the Constitution give to the people?

    It is the highest law of the land.

C   The Three Parts of the Constitution

1. The Preamble is the introduction to the document. It tells the purposes of the Constitution.

2. The Document has seven articles. It tells the powers and the responsibilities of the three branches of federal government.

3. The twenty-six amendments are changes to the Constitution. They give rights to the people.

D   Circle the words.

1. The U.S. Constitution has | three / seven | parts.

2. The | Preamble / Document | is the introduction to the Constitution.

3. It tells | the rights of the states. / the purposes of the Constitution.

4. The Document has | three / seven | articles.

5. It tells the | documents and amendments / powers and responsibilities | of the | three / ten |

    branches of | national / local | government.

6. Today there are twenty-six | articles / amendments | to the Constitution.

7. Amendments are | changes. / introductions.

8. Some of the amendments | give rights to / limit the freedoms of | the people.

E   The Preamble to the Constitution

Here is the Preamble (introduction) to the U.S. Constitution. The first line is the real words. The second line is the meaning.

We the people of the United States,

in order to form a more perfect Union,
to have a better country,

establish justice,
be fair,

insure domestic tranquility,
have peace at home,

provide for the common defense,
protect the country,

promote the general welfare,
give the people good lives,

and secure the blessings of liberty
and give freedom

to ourselves and   our posterity
                      our children

do ordain and establish
are making

this Constitution for the United States of America.

F   Make sentences from this sentence pattern.

EXAMPLE: One purpose of the U.S. Constitution is to have a better country.

One purpose of the U.S. Constitution is to _____.

G The Document

The Document of the U.S. Constitution has seven articles.

Article 1:   the legislative branch of federal government
Article 2:   the executive branch of federal government
Article 3:   the judicial branch of federal government
Article 4:   the states and the federal government
Article 5:   how to amend (change) the Constitution
Article 6:   how the Constitution is the highest law of the land
Article 7:   how to make the Constitution law

H Make sentences with this sentence pattern.

EXAMPLE: Article 1 is about the Legislative Branch of government.

Article _____ is about _____.
　　　　(number)

I The Amendments

The first ten amendments to the Constitution are the Bill of Rights. They tell about the freedoms of the people. Some of the other amendments are about the national government.

Amendment 12:   The people will vote separately for President and Vice President.

Amendment 16:   The government can put a tax on people's income.

Amendment 20:   New Presidents will take office (begin their job) on January 20.

Amendment 22:   A President can serve only two terms (eight years).

Amendment 25:   The Vice President will do the President's job if the President can't do it.

J Make sentences with this sentence pattern.

EXAMPLE: Amendment 12 says that the people will vote separately for President and Vice President.

Amendment _____ says that _____.
　　　　　(number)

Module 6B: Basic Rights and Freedoms

 A **Vocabulary**

Constitutional
Convention

Congress

freedom of speech

freedom of
the press

freedom of
religion

freedom of
assembly

weapons

soldiers

search

search warrant

trial
(court)

jury

lawyer

protection

cruel
punishment

The Bill of Rights

At the Constitutional Convention of 1787, representatives of twelve new states wrote the U.S. Constitution. The Constitution became the law of the land in 1788. But some Americans were unhappy with it because it didn't give the people rights and freedoms. The Congress (the Legislative Branch of government) added amendments (changes) to the Constitution. The first ten amendments are the Bill of Rights.

Amendment 1:   freedom of speech, the press, religion, and assembly (the right to meet)

Amendment 2:   the right to have weapons

Amendment 3:   protection against soldiers in homes

Amendment 4:   protection against police searches (without a search warrant)

Amendments 5, 6, and 7:   the right to a trial in court with a jury and a lawyer

Amendment 8:   protection against cruel punishment

Amendment 9:   gives other rights to the people, even if they are not in the Constitution

Amendment 10:   gives powers not in the Constitution to the states or the people

 Make sentences with this sentence pattern.

EXAMPLE: Amendment 1 gives the people freedom of speech.

| Amendment(s) _____ (number) | give(s) the people | the right
freedom
protection | _____. |

D Tell about the freedoms, rights, and protections shown in the pictures. In each box, write the number of the amendment.

EXAMPLE: Amendment 3 gives the people protection against soldiers in their homes.

E Other Amendments

Some of the other amendments to the U.S. Constitution give special rights to groups of people. Here are some examples.

Amendment 13 ended slavery in the United States.

Amendment 14 gave all people born in the United States or naturalized the right of citizenship.

Amendment 15 gave black people the right to vote.

Amendment 19 gave women the right to vote.

Amendment 23 gave residents of Washington, D.C. the right to vote for President and Vice President.

Amendment 26 gave all citizens eighteen and over the right to vote.

F **Circle *yes* or *no*. On the line, write the number of the amendment. (You can look back at pages 70 and 71.)**

1. Can people in the United States have slaves?   yes   (no)   _13_

2. Can women vote in elections?   yes   no   ___

3. Can black people vote?   yes   no   ___

4. Can people in the United States go to church?   yes   no   ___

5. Must they take soldiers into their homes?   yes   no   ___

6. Can they have weapons?   yes   no   ___

7. If they go to trial, can they have a lawyer and a jury?   yes   no   ___

8. Can residents of Washington, D.C. vote for President and Vice President?   yes   no   ___

9. Must people in the United States let the police into their homes for a search without a search warrant?   yes   no   ___

10. Can sixteen-year-old citizens vote?   yes   no   ___

11. Can people meet to talk about the government?   yes   no   ___

12. Can the courts or the police give people cruel punishment?   yes   no   ___

13. Can people in the United States tell their ideas in newspapers?   yes   no   ___

14. Do the people have other rights?   yes   no   ___

15. Do the states have powers?   yes   no   ___

G **Do the people of the United States have other freedoms, rights, and protections? Tell the class about them.**

H **Do people in your native country have the same freedoms, rights, and protections? Tell the class.**

The Federal Government

Module 7A: Overview of U.S. Government

A The Government of the United States

The government of the United States is the federal (national) government. The United States is a republic because the people elect (choose) representatives. It is also a democracy because the people have the power.

Political parties choose candidates for office. Only U.S. citizens can vote in elections. The voters choose the President and Vice President of the United States. They also elect senators and representatives from their state, the governor of their state, the mayor of their city, and other government officials. These officials represent the people.

B Circle the words.

1. The | state / federal | government is the national government of the United States.

2. The United States is a | republic / petition | and a | constitution. / democracy.

3. In a republic, the voters | make the laws. / elect representatives.

4. In a democracy, the people have | the power. / no rights.

5. Only | permanent residents / U.S. citizens | can vote in | elections. / branches of government.

6. They choose the | President and Vice President. / INS officials.

7. The people also vote for | federal laws / senators and representatives | from their state.

8. The voters also elect | their state governor and city mayor. / the President's Cabinet.

C Match the sentence parts. Draw lines.

1. Political parties   elect officials.

2. The voters   represent the voters.

3. Elected officials   choose candidates for office.

D The Branches of the Federal Government

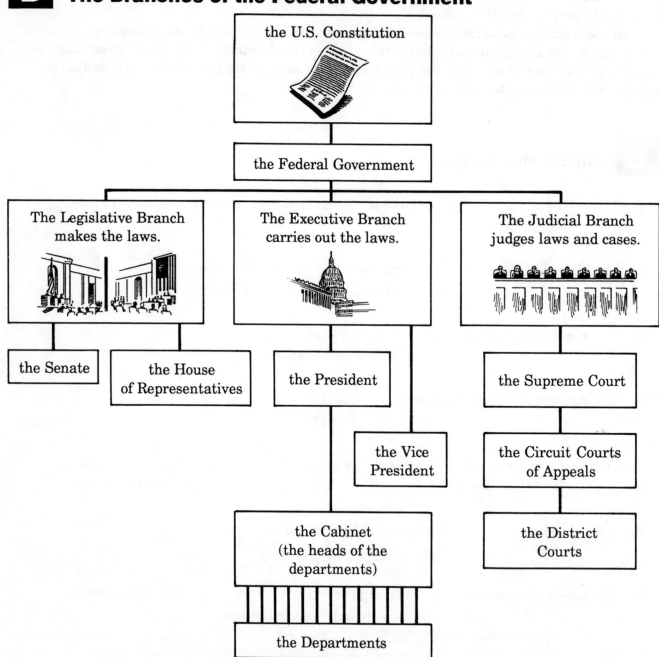

In the system of checks and balances, each branch has some power over the other two branches.

E Make sentences with this sentence pattern.

EXAMPLE: The Senate is in the legislative branch (of the federal government).

| The | Senate
House of Representatives
President
Vice President
Cabinet
Departments
Supreme Court
Circuit Courts of Appeal
District Courts | is
are | in the | legislative
executive
judicial | branch. |

F Write the answers from D.

1. What document has more power than the federal government? *the Constitution*

2. What are the three branches of government? _____

   _____

3. What are the two houses (parts) of the legislative branch? _____

   _____

4. Who are the two highest officials of the executive branch? _____

   _____

5. What is the President's Cabinet? _____

6. What is the highest court in the judicial branch of the federal government? _____

   _____

7. What courts are lower than the Circuit Courts of Appeals? _____

G   Political Parties

The first political parties were the Federalists and the Democratic-Republicans. At the time of President George Washington, the Federalists wanted more power for the federal government. The other party opposed a strong national government. The Democratic-Republicans became the Democratic Party of today.

There were many political parties in the past, and there are many political parties today. But there are only two big, important parties. These are the Democrats and the Republicans. The President of the United States always belongs to one of these two parties. President Bush and Vice President Quayle are Republicans.

Many Americans belong to political parties, usually the Democratic or the Republican Party. There are local, state, and national groups for each party.

H   Write the party names from the box on the lines.

Federalists	Democrats
Democratic-Republicans	Republicans

1. The first political parties were the _____ and the _____.

2. The _____ wanted more power for the federal government.

3. At the time of George Washington, the _____ wanted less government power.

4. The _____ became the Democratic Party.

5. The two big, important political parties today are the _____ and the _____.

6. The President and Vice President of the United States are always _____ or _____.

7. Now the President and Vice President are _____.

8. Most Americans today are _____ or _____.

State Government

Module 8A: Branches of Government and Officials

A The Federal and State Government

State government is like the federal government in many ways, but there are a few differences.

State government:	The federal government:
• is in the form of a republic because the people elect representatives.	• is in the form of a republic because the people elect representatives.
• is a democracy because the people have the power.	• is a democracy because the people have the power.
• follows the state constitution with its bill of rights.	• follows the U.S. Constitution with its Bill of Rights.
• has three branches: the legislative, the executive, and the judicial.	• has three branches: the legislative, the executive, and the judicial.
• gives different powers to the three branches.	• gives different powers to the three branches.
The legislative branch of state government:	The legislative branch of the federal government:
• usually has two houses.* The upper house is a senate, and the lower house is a state assembly or house of representatives.	• has two houses. The upper house is the Senate, and the lower house is the House of Representatives.
• makes state laws.	• makes federal laws.
The executive branch of state government:	The executive branch of the federal government:
• has the governor and lieutenant governor as leaders.	• has the President and Vice President as leaders.
• includes advisors to the governor. Sometimes the people elect the advisors, and sometimes the governor appoints them.	• includes advisors to the President in the Cabinet. The Secretaries are the heads of departments.
• includes commissions, boards, and departments.	• includes federal agencies.

* Only Nebraska has a one-house state legislature.

The judicial branch of state government:
- has different levels of courts.
- judges cases of state law.
- includes a state supreme court.
- can include appellate, county, superior, district, circuit, municipal, and special courts.

The judicial branch of the federal government:
- has different levels of courts.
- judges cases of federal law.
- includes the U.S. Supreme Court.
- includes Circuit Courts of Appeal and District Courts.

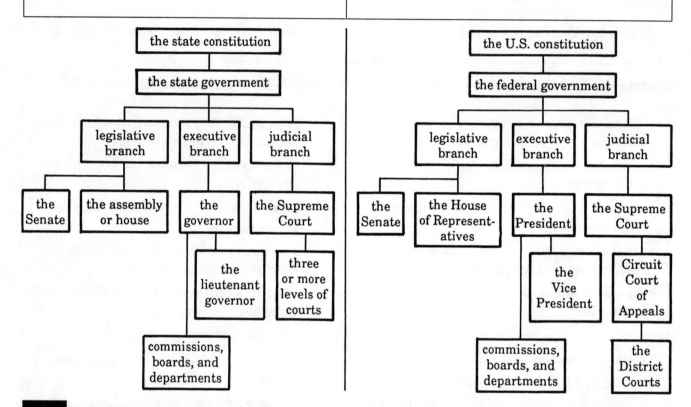

B   Make sentences about the similarities in state and federal government with this sentence pattern.

EXAMPLE: Both state and federal government are in the form of a republic because the people elect representatives.

Both state and federal government _____.

C   Make sentences about the differences in state and federal government with this sentence pattern.

State government follows a state constitution, but the federal government follows the U.S. Constitution.

State government _____, but the federal government _____.

The Legislative Branch of the State Government of California

The California state legislature has two houses. They are the Senate and the Assembly. There are forty senators in the Senate and eighty assemblymen in the Assembly. Senators stay in office for four years. Assemblymen stay in office for two years.

In California, the voters elect legislators by senatorial district and by assembly district. My state senator is Newton Russell. He is a Republican. My state assemblyman is Phillip Wyman. He is a Republican, too.

 Write the information about California or your state and your district on the lines.

The _____ state legislature has two houses. They are the state Senate and
    (Name of state)

the _____. There are _____ senators in the Senate and _____
    (Name of lower house)   (number)   (number)

_____ in the _____. Senators stay in
(assemblymen?   representatives?)   (Name of lower house)

office for _____ years. _____ stay in office for _____ years.
           (number)   (Assemblymen?   Representatives?)   (number)

In _____, the voters elect legislators by _____.
    (Name of state)   (population? district? the whole state?)

My state senator is _____. He/She is a _____.
                        (Name)   (Political party)

My state _____ is _____. He/She
            (assemblyman? representative?)   (Name)

is a _____.
    (Political party)

The Executive Branch of the State Government of California

In <u>California</u>, <u>George Deukmejian</u> is the governor. He is a <u>Republican</u>. The lieutenant governor is <u>Leo McCarthy</u>, a <u>Democrat</u>. The governor stays in office for <u>four</u> years. <u>March Fong Yu</u> is the <u>Secretary of State.</u> She is an <u>elected</u> official.

G **Write the information about California or your state on the lines.**

In _____, _____ is the governor. He is a _____.
    (State)   (Name)   (Political party)

The lieutenant governor is _____, a _____. The governor
                             (Name)   (Political party)

stays in office for _____ years. _____ is the _____.
                 (number)   (Name)   (Name of Office)

He/She is an _____ official.
         (elected? appointed?)

 The Judicial Branch of the State Government of California

In California, the highest court is the Supreme Court. There is <u>only one</u> state <u>Supreme Court</u>, but it meets in <u>Los Angeles</u>, <u>San Francisco</u>, and <u>Sacramento</u>. It has <u>one</u> chief justice and <u>six</u> judges. <u>The governor appoints them, and then the people vote on the appointments.</u> They are Supreme Court justices for <u>twelve</u> years.

I **Answer these questions about California's or your state's court system.**

1. What is the highest court? How many courts of this kind are there?

2. Where does it meet? How many judges does it have?

3. Does the governor appoint the judges or do the people elect them?

4. For how many years is a person a judge in this court?

5. What other kinds of courts are there?

Local Government

Module 9A: County and City Services

A Vocabulary

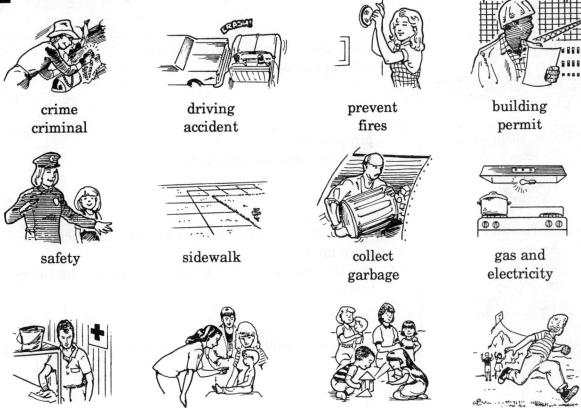

crime
criminal

driving
accident

prevent
fires

building
permit

safety

sidewalk

collect
garbage

gas and
electricity

sanitation
cleanliness

health
clinic

childcare

recreation

B Public Services

Most city governments provide public services. But in small towns, the county government sometimes provides the services for the people. Often, cities and counties work together. Governments usually serve the people through city or county departments. Here are some departments and their services.

Department	Services
Police	• tries to keep the city safe from crime and to catch criminals • tries to make driving safe and checks into accidents

Fire	• fights fires • helps people to prevent fires
Building and Safety	• gives building permits • checks building safety
Public Works	• takes care of streets and sidewalks • collects garbage
Public Utilities	• provides water • often provides gas and electricity
Public Health and Sanitation	• checks places like restaurants and nursing homes for cleanliness • provides free or low-cost health clinics and gives information about health
Human or Social Services	• helps poor people with money, housing, jobs, and childcare
Parks and Recreation	• provides places for recreation • takes care of parks

C Circle the words.

1. Most city governments provide | public services.
                                    | free housing.

2. In small towns, the | state | government can provide services.
                         | county |

3. Governments usually serve the people through | representatives.
                                                   | departments.

Make sentences about the information in A with this sentence pattern.

EXAMPLE: The Police Department of a city or county usually tries to keep the city safe from crime and catch criminals.

The _____ Department of a city or county usually

(Name of department)

_____.

(service)

 How to Find Public Services

Most city and county governments provide similar services, but the names of the offices are sometimes different. You can find the names, addresses, and telephone numbers of government offices in your local telephone book. They are together in the front part of the white pages. The offices are usually in a list under the title "City Government Offices" or "County Government Offices" and the name of the city or county. Here are examples from a city near Los Angeles, California.

CULVER CITY CITY OF 9770 Culver Bl CC	
GENERAL INFORMATION	837 5211
Building Safety	202 5806
Fire Dept 4010 Dequesne Av CC	
Business Calls	202 5800
Emergency Calls	911
Or	839 1146
HEALTH DEPARTMENT	555 9089
HUMAN SERVICES	202 5695
LIBRARY PUBLIC	
Culver City 4975 Overland Av CC	559 1676
MUNICIPAL BUS LINES 9815 Jefferson Bl CC	559 8310
Closed Weekends & Holidays	
PARKS & RECREATION DIVISION	
General Office 4117 Overland Av CC	202 5689

POLICE DEPT 4040 Duquesne Av CC	
Business Calls	837 1221
Emergency Calls Only	911
Or	837 6161
PUBLIC WORKS INSPECTORS	202 5711
PURCHASING	202 5714
SANITATION DEPARTMENT	202 5727
SCHOOL—PUBLIC	
Look Under Name Of School	
School District See Culver City Unified School District	
SENIOR CITIZENS CENTER 4153 Overland Av CC	202 5856
Or	559 2266
SENIOR CITIZENS INFORMATION REFERRAL SERVICE	
4153 Overland Av CC	837 6333
STREETS DEPARTMENT	202 5703
TRAFFIC COURT	836 7042
UTILITIES	555 1000

F **Write the words from the box.**

city or county	County Goverment Offices	white pages
telephone book	City Government Offices	

You can find the names, addresses, and telephone numbers of government offices in the front part of the _____ of your local _____. The offices are usually in a list under the title "_____" or "_____" and the name of the _____.

What government office should you call in these situations? On the first line, write the name of the department from the telephone list in E. On the second line, write the name, address, and telephone number of the department in your city or county. (Look in your local telephone book.)

1. You have an accident.

   Culver City   Your City

   _____   _____   _____   _____
   Department   Department   Address   Telephone

2. There is a fire in your apartment building.

   Culver City   Your City

   _____   _____   _____   _____
   Department   Department   Address   Telephone

3. You want to know about the safety of your apartment building.

   Culver City   Your City

   _____   _____   _____   _____
   Department   Department   Address   Telephone

4. The sidewalk on your street needs repair.

   Culver City   Your City

   _____   _____   _____   _____
   Department   Department   Address   Telephone

5. There is no water or gas in your building.

   Culver City   Your City

   _____   _____   _____   _____
   Department   Department   Address   Telephone

6. You have three children but no money, home, or job.

   Culver City   Your City

   _____   _____   _____   _____
   Department   Department   Address   Telephone

7. You want to know about places to go for recreation.

   Culver City   Your City

   _____   _____   _____   _____
   Department   Department   Address   Telephone

Module 10A: Overview of U.S. History

A **Work in pairs. Look only at this page. Ask your partner about a missing date. Write the date on the line. Then answer your partner's question.**

EXAMPLES: Student 1: When did Columbus discover North America?
Student 2: Columbus discovered North America in 1492.
When did the thirteen colonies declare their independence from England?
Student 1: They declared their independence in 1776.

Columbus discovered North America.

_1492_

The thirteen colonies declared their independence from England.
America won the Revolutionary War.

1776
_1787_

The United States expanded to the Pacific Ocean.

by 1853

Many European immigrants came to the United States.

_1840_

During the Civil War, President Lincoln freed the slaves with the Emancipation Proclamation.

1863

The United States entered the First World War. After the war women got the right to vote.

_1917_
1920

Many Americans were out of work during the Great Depression.

_1930_

After the Second World War, the Cold War between the United States and the Soviet Union began.

the 1950's

Americans fought against segregation in the Civil Rights Movement.

The United States entered the Space Age and the Computer Age.

the 1960's

A **Work in pairs. Look only at this page. Answer your partner's question. Then ask your partner about a missing date. Write the date on the line.**

EXAMPLES: Student 1: When did Columbus discover North America?
Student 2: Columbus discovered North America in 1492.
When did America win the Revolutionary War?
Student 1: America won the war in 1781.

Columbus discovered North America.   **1492**

The thirteen colonies declared their independence
from England.   *1776*

America won the Revolutionary War.   **1781**

The United States expanded to the Pacific Ocean.   *1853*

Many European immigrants came to the United
States.   **the 1840's**

During the Civil War, President Lincoln freed the
slaves with the Emancipation Proclamation.   *1863*

The United States entered the First World War.   **1917**
After the war women got the right to vote.   *1920*

Many Americans were out of work during the
Great Depression.   **the 1930's**

After the Second World War, the Cold War between the United States and the Soviet Union
began.   *1950*

Americans fought against segregation in the Civil
Rights Movement.   **the 1960's**

The United States entered the Space Age and the
Computer Age.   *1960*

B Circle the words. Then number the pictures in time order 1-6.

☐

The thirteen colonies declared their independence from
| slavery.
| England.

☐

Many | European immigrants | came to the United States.
| Spanish colonists

☐

Columbus discovered | North America.
| China.

☐

The United States expanded to the
| border of the Soviet Union.
| Pacific Ocean.

☐

During the Civil War, Lincoln freed the slaves with the
| Declaration of Independence.
| Emancipation Proclamation.

☐

America won the | Revolutionary | War.
| Civil

Write the words from the box on the lines. Then number the pictures in time order 9–16.

1 Cold War	3 First World War	5 right to vote
2 Space Age	4 Great Depression	6 the Civil Rights Movement

☐ The United States entered the ___3___ _____.

☐ Many Americans were out of work during the ___4___.

☐ After the Second World War, the ___1___ between the United States and the Soviet Union began.

☐ After the war women got the ___5___.

☐ Americans fought against segregation in ___6___.

☐ The United States entered the ___2___ and the Computer Age.

 Work in pairs. Tell the class two events in U.S. history. The class will name the first (earlier) event.

Module 11A: Important State Events

A **Work in pairs. Look only at this page. Ask your partner about a missing date. Write the date on the line. Then answer your partner's question.**

EXAMPLE: Student 1: When did only Indians live in California?
Student 2: Before 1542. When did white men from Spain come to San Diego Bay?

Only Indians lived in California.	
White men from Spain came to San Diego Bay.	1542
Spain claimed the land of California.	
Spanish missionaries came to teach religion to the Indians.	in the 1700's
Mexico declared its independence from Spain. Mexico claimed California.	
The United States won California in a war with Mexico.	1847
John Marshall discovered gold in California. The Gold Rush began.	
Many people came to California by train.	after 1869
There was a big earthquake in San Francisco.	
The population (number of people) of California grew quickly.	in the 1900's

Work in pairs. Look only at this page. Answer your partner's question. Then ask your partner about a missing date. Write the date on the line.

EXAMPLE: Student 1: When did only Indians live in California?
                   Student 2: Before 1542. When did white men from Spain come to San Diego Bay?

	Only Indians lived in California.	**before 1542**
	White men from Spain came to San Diego Bay.	
	Spain claimed the land of California.	**1769**
	Spanish missionaries came to teach religion to the Indians.	
	Mexico declared its independence from Spain. Mexico claimed California.	**1822**
	The United States won California in a war with Mexico.	
	John Marshall discovered gold in California. The Gold Rush began.	**1846**
	Many people came to California by train.	
	There was a big earthquake in San Francisco.	**1906**
	The population (number of people) of California grew quickly.	

B Circle the words. Then number the pictures 1–6 in the correct time order.

☐   Before 1542, only │ Indians
                        │ Europeans │ lived in California.

☐   Then the first white men came to │ San Diego Bay.
                                      │ Sacramento.

[1] In the 1700s, Spanish │ slaves
                            │ missionaries │

     came to teach the │ immigrants │ religion.
                        │ Indians   │

☐   John Marshall discovered │ gold   │ in California in 1846.
                              │ the ocean │

☐   In the 1860s, many people came to California by │ train.
                                                     │ plane.

☐   In 1906, there was a big │ gold rush
                              │ earthquake │

     in San Francisco.

C Write the name of each country on two lines.

Spain	Mexico	the United States

1. The first white men in California were from _____Spain_____.

2. In 1769, _____ claimed the land of California.

3. Then _____ declared its independence from Spain.

4. In 1822, _____ claimed California.

5. In 1847, _____ won California in a war with Mexico.

6. Many people from other states in _____ came to California by train after 1869.

D Work in pairs. Tell the class two events in California history. The class will name the first (earlier) event.

E Finish this sentence about the history of California or your state in many ways.

EXAMPLE: On March 6, 1836, the Mexican army of General Santa Anna won the battle of the Alamo against the American settlers.

_____, _____ _____.
(date)   (person or people)   (action)

F With the class, write some important events of the history of your state here.

1. _____

2. _____

3. _____

4. _____

5. _____

6. _____

Module 12A: Important Local Events

A **Work in pairs. Look only at this page. Ask your partner about a missing date. Write the date on the line. Then answer your partner's question.**

EXAMPLES: Student 1: When did Gaspar de Portola and a group of Spaniards come to the area of Los Angeles?

Student 2: In 1769. When did the governor of California for Spain begin the pueblo of Los Angeles?

 Gaspar de Portola and a group of Spaniards came to the area of Los Angeles.

The governor of California for Spain began the pueblo (town) of Los Angeles.

1781

 The Gold Rush began in California, and many people came to Los Angeles.

The first train left Los Angeles for San Francisco.

1876

 Workers discovered oil in Los Angeles.

Work began on Los Angeles Harbor.

1899

 For the first time, the L.A. Aquaduct (pipeline) brought water to the city from other parts of California.

Los Angeles became the largest city in California.

1920

 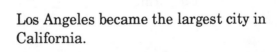 The first freeway (now the Pasadena Freeway) opened.

Los Angeles began the celebration of its two hundredth birthday.

1980

Work in pairs. Look only at this page. Answer your partner's question. Then ask your partner about a missing date. Write the date on the line.

EXAMPLES: Student 1: When did Gaspar de Portola and a group of Spaniards come to the area of Los Angeles?

Student 2: In 1769. When did the governor of California for Spain begin the pueblo of Los Angeles?

Gaspar de Portola and a group of Spaniards came to the area of Los Angeles.	**1769**
The governor of California for Spain began the pueblo (town) of Los Angeles.	
The Gold Rush began in California, and many people came to Los Angeles.	**1848**
The first train left Los Angeles for San Francisco.	
Workers discovered oil in Los Angeles.	**1893**
Work began on Los Angeles Harbor.	
For the first time, the L.A. Aquaduct (pipe line) brought water to the city from other parts of California.	**1913**
Los Angeles became the largest city in California.	
The first freeway (now the Pasadena Freeway) opened.	**1940**
Los Angeles began the celebration of its two hundredth birthday.	

Tell the important events in the history of Los Angeles from the pictures and words.

EXAMPLE: Gaspar de Portola and a group of Spaniards came to the area of Los Angeles in 1769.

1. 1769

Gaspar de Portola
a group of Spaniards

2. 1781

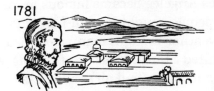

the governor of California
the pueblo of Los Angeles

3. 1848

the Gold Rush
many people

4. 1876

the first train
Los Angeles / San Francisco

5. 1893

discovered oil

6. 1899

Los Angeles Harbor

7. 1913

the L.A. Aquaduct
brought water

8. 1920

the largest city

9. 1940

the first freeway

10. 1980

200th birthday
celebration

 With the class, write some important events in the history of your town or city here.

1. _____

2. _____

3. _____

4. _____

5. _____

D Why Did the City Grow?

Los Angeles grew because of oil, cars, movies, farms, land, and sunshine. Workers discovered oil in 1893, and the invention of the car made oil important. The movie industry began in 1911, and Los Angeles became famous for movie stars. Soon aquaducts brought water to the farms, and many people bought land in Los Angeles. Other industries, universities (like U.C.L.A.), and the good weather brought many more people. Now Los Angeles has the largest land area of any city in the United States. It is one of the biggest cities in population. But it also has too much traffic (cars) and smog (bad air) and it has earthquakes.

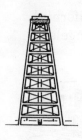    

E Circle the important things in the history of Los Angeles.

(gold)	oil	waterpipelines	freeways	movies
lakes	flags	movie stars	elephants	slaves
(cars)	smog	religion	Pilgrims	earthquakes
turkey	rain	the weather	fireworks	universities

F Match the sentence parts. Draw lines.

1. The invention of the car   made L.A. famous for stars.

2. The movie industry   aquaducts brought water.

3. People bought land because   brought traffic and smog.

4. Many people came to L.A.   to work and study.

5. The city of Los Angeles is   made oil important.

6. The growth of the city   large in area and population.

G Answer this question about Los Angeles. If you live in another city, answer the question about your city.

Why did the city grow?